Tickle Your Fancy

A Woman's Guide to Sexual Self-Pleasure

Sadie Allison

Illustrated by Steve Lee

Author: Sadie Allison
Editor: David Agnew
Creative Director: Richard G. Martinez
Design: LowbrowLabs.com

Illustrator: Steve Lee
Logo Design: Todd La Rose
Author Photo: Beau Bonneau
Cover Photo: Richard G. Martinez

Published by Tickle Kitty Press
3701 Sacramento Street PMB #107
San Francisco, CA 94118
United States
Fax: 1-(415) 876-1900
http://www.ticklekitty.com

Tickle Your Fancy: A Woman's Guide to Sexual Self-Pleasure
Copyright © 2001 by Tickle Kitty Press
All rights reserved
Third print
ISBN 0-9706611-0-X
Printed in Canada
Library of Congress Card Number: 00-193472

A Word of Caution

The purpose of this book is to educate. It is not intended to give medical or psychological therapy. As always, if you experience physical or mental complications, please consult a physician immediately. The author, illustrator and publisher shall have neither liability nor responsibility to any person or entity with respect to loss, damage, injury, or aliment caused or alleged to be caused directly or indirectly by the information or lack of information in this book.

Table of Contents

Introduction

Historically, women have received mixed, even negative messages about masturbation. Even today, society conditions women to think masturbation is harmful, sinful and abnormal. Adults told us, when we were little girls, masturbation was bad and sometimes punished us for doing it. Overall, this repression of female masturbation promoted sexual insecurities, shame, guilt and fear. However, society is beginning to understand and accept that women across the world practice masturbation as a perfectly normal, healthy activity.

Tickle Your Fancy: A Woman's Guide to Sexual Self-Pleasure is a how-to guide that explains and details everything from the basics of getting started with masturbation to more advanced tips and techniques for enhancing sexual self-pleasure.

This guide helps women understand and embrace their natural ability to enjoy sexual self-pleasure without guilt or inhibitions. It discusses why masturbation is healthy and offers

step-by-step instructions on a wide variety of techniques. Instructional diagrams and illustrations throughout the book will guide you in your learning process.

The first half of *Tickle Your Fancy* focuses on background and preparation information; the second half explains masturbation techniques and how to use popular sex toys.

There is no right, wrong or best way to masturbate. Every woman will have her unique preference and style—have patience and take time to discover what feels good to you. The techniques and recommendations offered in this book won't be pleasurable for everyone—experiment at your discretion and stop if anything causes you pain, discomfort or irritation. Always use caution when playing with sex toys, and of course practice good cleanliness and safety habits.

This book is for all women—no matter their age, relationship status or sexual orientation. It's possible that you're exploring your sexuality for the first time or that you've got an experienced hand and are looking for new ways to play. Whatever the reason, you found this book and should be commended for it. You are on your way to the endless possibilities of self-pleasure!

Think of this guide as your big sister, answering all your questions at length. It will alleviate your fears, introduce you to new techniques and help you develop a positive image of your body. If masturbation is new to you, the key is to openly explore it and give yourself time. Release your sexual inhibitions, have fun and enjoy yourself. Happy self-loving! ♥

1 Masturbation is Healthy

Masturbation is the first natural sex activity for most women. Biologically, we were meant to experience sexual pleasure with and without a partner. As children, we touch ourselves and learn that stimulating our genitals gives sensual pleasure, but it isn't until late childhood or adolescence that we recognize such behavior as "sexual."

~∽♡℮~

Still, those who don't discover masturbation as children can develop it as a learned skill. The problem is, some women don't take the time to explore their full sexual potential. Some claim, "I tried it before and didn't enjoy it," never indulging again. Lack of knowledge or persistence might cause such resistance. When you had sex for the first time, was it completely enjoyable? The first time you ate spinach or

masturbation:

The stimulation or manipulation of one's own genitals, often resulting in orgasm or sexual self-gratification. For women, masturbation generally consists of stimulating the genital area and clitoris. Sex aids or sex toys, including a variety of dildos, vibrators and other unique devices, are often used to enhance pleasure.

sushi, did you really like the taste? Maybe, but probably not. Masturbation is no different: Just as you acquire taste for new food, you can learn to like masturbation. And just as your culinary tastes might develop over time, your preferred masturbation techniques will likely change also.

Masturbation helps you explore your sexuality, allowing you to harmlessly discover and fulfill your sexual needs and desires. Regardless of race, age, marital status or orientation, masturbation can help you develop a strong sex life—mentally, emotionally and physically.

Jessica, 30, is an attractive, successful and single sales executive. She exercises four times a week at the gym near her office. She has a standing appointment with her manicurist and treats herself to a massage when she can afford it. She empowers herself to make her own decisions. As an independent woman, she would never dream of waiting for a man to come along and do something for her—except when it comes to sex. Her sexual desires are only fulfilled when she's involved in a relationship, completely relying on her partner for all her sexual needs. She's even spent years in bad relationships just to preserve the sexual component.

Sounds ridiculous, doesn't it? Jessica isn't alone—many women still have old-fashioned ideas about fulfilling their sexual needs. But we all have sexual desires, so why should the lack of a partner deprive us from fulfilling our sexual desires? Why not take matters into your own hands?

For some couples, the climax of one partner means sex is over for both of them. The other partner might feel unfulfilled, cheated or both. When this occurs, women sometimes feel guilty expecting to have their needs met! We should never be ashamed or afraid

In 1972, the American Medical Association declared masturbation a normal sexual activity.

An estimated 10% to 15% of women don't pursue masturbation simply because they don't know what to do.

to voice our needs. Suppose you were hungry and anticipated a luxurious dinner for two all afternoon. But if, when the meal arrived, your date said he felt full after the salad, you would hardly forego your own hunger and say, "That's all right. As long as you're satisfied, I'm satisfied." If you're still hungry, say so—your sexual needs are as real and valid as your date's sex drive. You should be able to communicate your desires, as well as satisfy them, even if your partner is tired, indifferent or unavailable.

Some women fear masturbation will reduce the quality of their lovemaking with a partner. Others worry that it will over-stimulate them or condition them to respond only to a certain stimulus. But masturbation doesn't jeopardize a healthy sex life, nor is it only an alternative to sex. Quite often, it can greatly enhance your sex life—with or without a partner.

Masturbation is healthy because ...

it boosts your self-esteem. Masturbation can help you overcome personal inhibitions and fulfill your sexual desires, fueling your self-confidence and self-image.

it can help relationships. Just because two people choose to share their lives doesn't mean their

bodies share the same schedule. When sexual desires, levels of excitement or pace differ, sexual self-pleasure can fill the void.

it's consistent sex. Masturbation provides individuals with a sexual outlet during puberty, as well as between romances, marriages and divorce. With masturbation, you can remain sexually active your entire life—always on your schedule and as frequently as you like!

it improves communication. Once you know exactly where and how you like to be stimulated, you can communicate these desires to your partner. You can show your partner what you like by guiding their hands and/or demonstrating yourself.

there are physiological benefits. Regular orgasms induce a state of peaceful relaxation by releasing your body's pleasure chemicals, called endorphins, from the brain. This process may help alleviate menstrual cramps and promote better sleeping.

it's safe sex. With the proper use of sex toys and good hygiene, masturbation reduces the possibility of acquiring or transmitting sexually transmitted diseases (STDs), including HIV and other common viruses transferred between sex partners.

you can choose to be abstinent. If you refrain from sexual activities with others, masturbation provides sexual release without the need for a partner.

it overcomes physical constraints. You can still enjoy sexual pleasure, even if your partner becomes ill or physically disabled. ♥

2 The Female Anatomy

The female body is one of nature's most beautiful works of art. Both sexes commonly express appreciation for a woman's soft skin, graceful curves and sensuality. Accordingly, it's important that women completely understand their own bodies both sexually and sensually. By getting comfortable with the proper terminology for the touch-sensitive parts of your body, you'll enhance your understanding of sexual stimulation. These erogenous zones, found in many different areas of the body, aren't limited to your outer sexual organs, genitals or vulva. If you stimulate these areas in certain ways, you can become sexually excited or aroused.

7

erogenous zones:

Areas of the body that are sensitive to touch and can be sexually gratifying. You can easily seduce yourself by touching and caressing your erogenous zones and discovering the good sensations created.

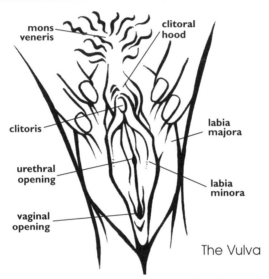

mons veneris

clitoral hood

clitoris

labia majora

urethral opening

labia minora

vaginal opening

The Vulva

vulva. A female's external genitals are referred to as the vulva. Collectively, the vulva consists of the labia minora and majora (inner and outer skin folds or "lips"), the tip of the clitoris ("clit"), the prepuce (clitoral foreskin or "hood"), two Bartholin's glands (which produce lubrication) and the urethral and vaginal openings. Vulvas come in a variety of different shapes, sizes and colors and vary greatly from one woman to the next.

labia majora and labia minora. The labia majora (i.e. the "outer lips") are folds of skin on the vulva's outermost parts. These folds contain fatty tissue and protect the inner vulva. The labia minora (i.e. the "inner lips") are thinner, smooth, parallel folds of skin inside the outer lips, serving to surround and also protect the inner vulva. Filled with nerve endings, the inner lips can be just as sensitive as the clitoris. The coloring ranges from bright red and pink to deep brown and black. Both labia majora and minora swell with blood during sexual arousal, reacting to touch and penetration as highly pleasurable erogenous zones.

clitoris. The clitoris, the nerve center for orgasm, is the primary source of sexual pleasure. Many women are unable to reach orgasm through intercourse alone, requiring some form of clitoral stimulation to achieve a climax. A very complex organ, the clitoris is comprised of a small glans or "head" (the visible portion of the clitoris), plus two clitoral shafts or "legs" (also called crura) that extend inward and straddle each side of the vaginal canal. The clitoris' other joining parts include the hood, inner lips, several bodies of tissue, muscles, nerve endings and networks of blood vessels. By stimulating some or all of these parts, orgasm can be achieved.

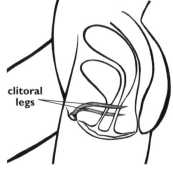

clitoral legs

The clitoris is the only organ in the human body whose sole purpose is to provide pleasure. Women were blessed with this erogenous zone and should take advantage of it!

The clitoris' head is located at the top of the vulva, hidden slightly under the hood, where the inner and outer labia meet. About the size of a pea, the clitoris can be viewed by gently parting the labia. The clitoris can also be compared to a penis, though it's obviously smaller in size. Like a penis, the clitoris has erectile tissue and a very high concentration of nerve endings. This highly sensitive organ swells with blood when sexually aroused, becoming erect and possibly doubling in size. Bringing the clitoris to this erect state during masturbation could help achieve orgasm. Its sensitivity to touch varies greatly between women.

hood and commissure. The hood is the area of skin formed by the joining of the inner lips over the clitoral head, which protects the clitoris. Found under the hood is an area of skin called the commissure. By gently pulling back on the outer lips and hood, you can expose the commissure. Many women enjoy direct

hood and commissure

stimulation of this sensitive area, finding it an effective way to achieve pleasurable arousal.

vagina. The vagina is an elastic canal that measures about three to four inches long, but could double in depth and width when aroused. Many women have vaginal orgasms, enjoying the pleasurable feelings of pressure, sexual fullness and stroking from various forms of penetration.

arousal:

To stir up or excite. It's a state of heightened physiological activity from sexual stimulation prior to sexual activity. When aroused, your body can produce natural lubrication. We sometimes describe these sensations as making us feel tingly, alive, warm, happy and radiant. Arousal can also produce a sense of well-being and euphoria.

mons veneris. Latin for "hill of Venus" (the Roman goddess of love), the mons veneris is the pad of fatty tissue and hair that sits on your pubic bone. The hair protects this area of your body, while the fatty tissue protects the pubic bone from impact during sexual intercourse.

urethra. When you urinate, urine flows from your bladder through a passageway called the urethra, eventually exiting from your body. The urethral opening, located between your clitoris and the vaginal opening, is sometimes called the "U-spot" and can be a highly sensitive erogenous zone.

g-spot. The G-spot, also known as the female prostate or urethral sponge, is a small mass of spongy tissue that surrounds the urethra. The G-spot is found inside the vagina, near the roof, about three quarters of the way up from the vaginal opening (right behind the pubic hair line). Made up of urethral glands, ducts and tissue, the G-spot is a highly pleasurable erogenous zone. This spongy tissue actually lies beside the vaginal canal and is stimulated by firm stroking and pressure felt through the vaginal wall.

In the early 1950s, German gynecologist Dr. Ernst Grafenberg was among the first to study and publish writings on this erotic pleasure region, hence the name "G-spot."

Normally, the G-spot is like a small spongy bean, about the size of a dime. After adequate stimulation, it becomes slightly hard and can swell to around the size of a quarter, protecting the urethra and acting as a buffer during sexual intercourse. When your G-spot is stimulated, you may feel the urge to pee, which is normal. G-spot stimulation can also lead to female ejaculation (see Chapter 3).

pelvic muscle. The pelvic muscle group, also called the PC or pubococcygeus muscles, extends around the anus, across the pelvic floor and attaches in front to the pubic bone in both women and men. When squeezing to stop yourself from urinating, the same muscles that "hold it in" are your pelvic muscles. This muscle group plays a very important role in masturbation and orgasm.

The Female Anatomy

For both women and men, these muscles contract involuntarily during sexual arousal and climax, starting out with random contractions during sexual play and arousal, then building into rhythmic contractions during orgasm.

It's estimated that 97% of females have masturbated by the age of 21.

You can strengthen your pelvic muscles using a technique known as Kegel exercises, increasing your sexual control and orgasmic intensity. Squeeze and release or flex your pelvic muscles to build muscle tone. You can make Kegels a part of your daily routine, practicing while you sit at your desk, drive your car or style your hair. If you exercise your pelvic muscles while masturbating, you'll better understand the feelings in your pelvic area, thus increasing your sensitivity and responsiveness.

nipples, areoles and breasts. Your nipples, areoles (the small rings of color around each nipple) and breasts can be important physical and physiological sources of pleasure. Stimulating the breasts and nipples could make them erect and sensitive, giving women sexual pleasure.

Women reach orgasm more frequently from masturbation than from any other sexual activity.

Some women experience orgasm from nipple stimulation alone, so don't neglect your nipples! Squeezing and caressing your breasts and nipples can delightfully enhance any masturbation session.

anal canal, rectum and sphincter muscles. Full of densely concentrated nerve endings, this erogenous zone can be quite sensitive to touch. The anus leads into the rectum and is composed of loose folds of soft, smooth tissue surrounded by sphincter muscles. Stimulating these nerve endings can be intensely pleasurable, even orgasmic. When the sphincter muscles relax, the tissue folds that make up the anal canal have a tremendous ability to expand, similar to the vaginal opening. It's sometimes hard to think of this region as an erotic zone, but it's a favorite pleasure area for many women. ♥

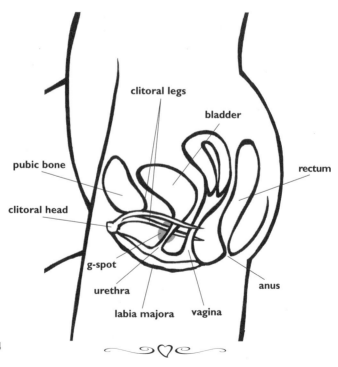

clitoral legs

bladder

pubic bone

rectum

clitoral head

g-spot

urethra

anus

labia majora

vagina

3

About
Orgasm

Orgasms occur at the peak of sexual arousal, radiating via the nervous system to all parts of the body. Basically, your body kicks into high gear: heart rates zoom up, respiration intensifies, blood pressure rises and the pelvic area and vulva throb at a euphoric peak. At this high level of sexual arousal, the body releases endorphins.

During orgasm, many people experience the following: pelvic muscle contractions, trembling and shaking, tingling skin, kicking reactions, tickling, slow-burning feelings, a sudden need to laugh (or even cry), plus many other sensations unique to each individual. Orgasms can be as mild as a peaceful sigh and a sensuous experience, saturating the body with warmth. Or sometimes, orgasms can be extremely intense, making you lose track of your surroundings for a short time.

orgasm:

The physical and emotional sensation experienced at the culmination of a sexual act such as intercourse or masturbation. Orgasm results from stimulation of the sexual organs. Biological orgasm, or "climax," is a sudden and intense release of tension from multiple, involuntary pleasurable pelvic muscle contractions within the vagina.

How do you know if you've experienced an orgasm? If your body moves or reacts in ways you didn't intend, while waves of pleasure run through your body with brief aftershocks, you're probably experiencing an orgasm. If it helps, compare an orgasm to a sneeze. When you have to sneeze, there's no turning back—the sneeze happens involuntarily and effortlessly. The orgasmic reflex works much in the same way. When you reach the point of no return, your pelvic muscles involuntarily contract.

About Orgasm

Virtually all women are capable of reaching orgasm, but many differ in their ability to achieve this state. For some women, orgasms occur easily. Others have orgasms as an

95% of women orgasm when they masturbate.

occasional treat. Some women never experience an orgasm. Yet modern sex therapists find it highly unlikely that this last group is physically incapable of orgasming, of being "anorgasmic." Instead, sex therapists prefer to call such women "pre-orgasmic"—they simply haven't had an orgasm yet.

And what do sex therapists usually prescribe for women who haven't orgasmed? Masturbation! It's a great way for women to figure out what arouses them sexually. In fact, women who've never achieved orgasm with a partner often have one on their own.

> *Jackie, a 43-year-old homemaker, has been married for 20 years. A mother of three, she's a role model in her community and is no prude. She enjoys a stiff drink, regularly downloads lewd jokes off the Internet and is usually the last to leave the dance floor. Yet, she and her husband have infrequent sex because his career as a consultant requires his absence for weeks or months at a time. Jackie considers her sex life very fulfilling, but she's never orgasmed—even while masturbating.*

Jackie and women like her probably haven't found what works for them. Many settle with their non-orgasmic relation-ships and think, "It's all right, it's not a big deal." But whether they admit it or not, almost every woman would like to experience orgasm. Remember: Even if you've got an inactive sexual relationship, you still have you! You can take control of your sex life.

Women have the right to feel comfortable exploring their own bodies and achieving sexual gratification, which includes having stronger orgasms more frequently. Reading guides such as this book, gradually learning to let yourself experience sexual self-pleasure, can be your prescription for orgasm.

If you've never orgasmed, don't expect to have one right away. As with most new activities, there is a learning curve. Your body might need several weeks to learn how to receive pleasure from your touch. Learning to orgasm—or how to orgasm more regularly—is no different.

Spend a little time every day masturbating without the expectation of orgasming. Your first orgasm might surprise you. Some women reach orgasm in a couple minutes or less; others take up to 20 minutes or more. However your body responds to sexual stimulation, enjoy pleasuring yourself and don't worry how long it takes for you to climax.

> *clitoral orgasms.* Filled with nerve endings, the clitoris is the primary source of sexual pleasure. It's also where the vast majority of orgasms are produced. While stimulating other areas could cause

an orgasm, it's usually some sort of clitoral stimulation that triggers climax. In fact, one or more parts of the clitoral network usually participate in achieving orgasm. For example, consistent stimulation of the inner labia or commissure can lead to orgasm.

vaginal orgasms. Vaginal penetration can cause vaginal orgasms without any direct clitoral stimulation. However, the clitoris almost always gets stimulated indirectly during vaginal penetration, contributing to vaginal orgasms. Penetration strokes the nerve endings of the clitoral legs, located along the walls of the vaginal canal, giving pleasurable sensations. In addition, penetration indirectly stimulates the head of the erect clitoris. The act of pushing and pulling the inner labia during penetration also lightly tugs on the clitoris itself. So while "vaginal orgasms" are possible, the complex clitoral structure works in unison to produce them.

g-spot orgasms. Stimulating the urethral sponge produces G-spot orgasms. By pressing up into your vagina's roof, you'll stimulate the G-spot tissue through the vaginal wall. Many women enjoy G-spot stimulation best after they've already had an orgasm, when the erectile tissue of both the genitals and G-spot is swollen and highly sensitive. This also makes it easier to locate the G-spot. While some women can orgasm from G-spot stimulation alone, many need simultaneous stimulation of the clitoris to achieve G-spot orgasm.

female ejaculation. Some women release fluid from their genitals during sexual climax, and this

It is estimated that about 10% of women ejaculate during orgasm. phenomenon of female ejaculation has been linked to sexual stimulation of the G-spot. When stimulated, the G-spot fills with blood and the surrounding glands fill with a clear fluid that's a substance similar to male semen—without the sperm. These glands, connected to the urethra, transport such fluid. It either seeps, flows or squirts out of the urethra during ejaculation. If you happen to be a woman who ejaculates, rest assured—it's a perfectly normal occurrence.

multiple and sequential orgasms. Multiple orgasms are two or more orgasms, back-to-back, without any break of stimulation between each climax. Restimulating yourself every few minutes or so achieves sequential orgasms. Many women enjoy several orgasms during a sexual experience; others may achieve just one. You may have a highly responsive clitoris, or you may become sensitive to the point that continued stimulation is no longer pleasurable. For some women, too much stimulation is painful. Whatever your preference, simply be aware of your body's potential so you can control just how many orgasms you enjoy during masturbation.

After an orgasm, the clitoris shrinks slightly but can be sexually rearoused immediately. Achieving multiple orgasms is an art within itself. It's all a matter of keeping an open mind as you explore, learn and practice. ♥

Getting Ready for Pleasure

Preparing for pleasure is an important part of any sexual experience. Whether planning for a solitary episode or one shared with a partner, get comfortable enough to free your mind and body.

Prepare your environment to help you relax and freely let go of your inhibitions. Disconnect your phone and turn off your cellular or pager. Accent your surroundings to create just the right ambiance and don't forget to gather any visual and sexual aids you might wish to use beforehand.

Setting the Mood

sound. Play something slow and romantic that makes you feel sexy and sensual, or play upbeat music to "pump yourself up." This is your private, personal time, so do whatever makes you feel comfortable.

candles and lighting. For a romantic ambiance, create an intimate environment by lighting candles or dimming the lights.

temperature. Warmer air may ignite your passions, but cooler air might heighten your sensitivity. Experiment and find out what works best for you.

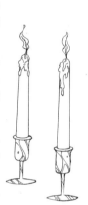

scent. Scented candles, perfumes, flowers or incense can provide intimate, subtle aromas to accent your surroundings.

location. Don't limit yourself to the bed or couch—sitting or standing in the bathtub or shower might be just as fun!

Take a Sensuous Bath

Taking a long hot bath can sensuously begin a self-loving experience. You can turn the bathroom into a romantic setting simply by adding candlelight. Enjoy your favorite scented soap, bubble bath, gel or oils. Use a soft sponge to bathe and soothe your body. Touch, caress and explore, gliding your hands over every erogenous zone.

Have a Look in the Mirror

Exploring your sexual anatomy in a mirror can build your sexual self-awareness. In a comfortable and private place, use a mirror to observe your body's contours and the uniqueness of your vulva and anus. Notice the shape, size and color. Lay back, gently part

Women are, in fact, three times more likely to orgasm from masturbation than from sexual intercourse.

your outer labia and admire your natural beauty. Flex your pelvic and sphincter muscles and observe the movements. Massage yourself and feel your body's natural reactions to touch. Freely enjoy the exploration of your sexual anatomy.

Trim, Shave and Shape

Shaving your legs, underarms and other body parts can make you look and feel sexy. Trimming and shaping your pubic hair can create an even more beautiful erogenous zone. You might be surprised how beautiful this area looks once you

groom it! Admiring yourself can spur your arousal or make you feel a bit more daring. Take time to appreciate your natural beauty.

There are many ways to groom yourself. A licensed aesthetician at a salon can give you a professional bikini wax. You can wax yourself at home using a depilatory cream or shave. When shaving, you can be creative—rectangle, triangle and diamond shapes are popular and fun—or you can go totally bald. But bear the following tips in mind when shaving your pubic area:

- ♥ Start by using hair-cutting scissors or an electric beard and mustache trimmer to trim your hair to a manageable length.

- ♥ Next, take a hot shower or place a hot washcloth over your vaginal area and moisten the hair to be removed.

- ♥ Apply shaving cream, gel or soap. To prevent stinging, don't let the products get inside your vagina.

- ♥ Using a new razor blade, delicately shave downward and inward in the direction that the hair grows.

- ♥ Take your time and use caution when you shave around the bikini line and outer labia.

- ♥ A gentle toner or astringent may prevent rashes after you shave.

Remember to Breathe

Like any other cardiovascular activity, achieving orgasm requires plenty of oxygen to fuel the body. During sexual arousal, your respiratory requirements increase as blood gets pumped into the genitals. Remember to breathe steadily, taking deep and regular breaths as your excitement builds.

Empty Your Bladder

Emptying your bladder before you masturbate should help make you relaxed and ready for pleasure. However, it's not necessary. Some women enjoy the added pressure of a full bladder on the nerve endings that promote orgasm. ♥

An estimated 30% of women climax only when they masturbate.

Tickle Your Fancy

5

Tickle Your Fancy

Fantasy
and Adult
Entertainment

Indulging in fantasy and adult entertainment can greatly enhance your imagination and sex drive, plus stimulate your erotic mind and visual sense using a variety of mediums. Your level of enjoyment could surprise you, and possibly motivate you to learn new techniques!

5 Fantasy

Any woman can weave her mind's sexual daydreams into erotic fantasies, intensifying her masturbation experiences. Fantasizing can fuel a healthy outlook and take you on private journeys. You're limited only by your own willingness to indulge. Dare to dream and allow your mind to go wherever it pleases. Be creative as you set the stage for fantasy, one of the greatest sexual aids at your disposal.

About 50% of females fantasize in conjunction with their masturbation experiences.

To begin your fantasy, close your eyes and picture yourself engaging in a sexual act you've always wanted to experience. Or maybe replay a hot sexual encounter you had in the past. If this proves difficult, remember a sexy scene in a movie that excited you and adapt that into your fantasy.

Not all fantasies must involve a sexually explicit act with another person, nor should you expect to actually perform such acts. That's why such dreams are called "fantasies." Also remember that many women don't fantasize at all when they masturbate, which is perfectly normal.

Erotic Literature

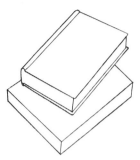

You can use erotic literature to educate yourself, learn new techniques and enhance fantasizing. Books and magazines about sex can both educate and titillate, giving you sexual ideas and inspiration. Female erotica by female authors might stir your mood, or perhaps the short "steamier" stories found in adult magazines are more your speed. Whatever your preference, major book stores and many Internet retailers offer erotic literature for easy purchase.

Adult Video

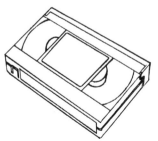

Adult cinema, also referred to as "X-rated movies," can be great sexual aids. Whatever your taste or desire, adult cinema has something for everyone. Adult videos are offered in many different categories: educational, softcore/hardcore, classic modern movies, themed (homosexual or bisexual), and many

5

others. Films with softer storylines and plots can accent your romantic ambiance, or you can try a more intense film with lots of sex scenes to get you aroused. To help choose an adult video to watch, read reviews or the text on the video boxes, ask friends for recommendations or look for award-winning films. Once you discover what works for you, try other movies made by the same director or producer or starring the same actors. Adult bookstores and video rental stores readily offer adult videos in adult movie sections. You can also subscribe to cable sex channels or purchase movies through mail-order catalogs and the Internet.

The Internet

The Internet has literally thousands of web sites dedicated to sex information, sex entertainment and erotic literature. The variety of sexual perspectives and resources available is tremendous. Individual web sites cater to virtually any topic you're interested in. The Internet commonly features: erotic photography, video and audio clips, discussion groups, advice columns and much, much more.

Women often obtain sex information or fantasy material on the Internet because it's private and often offers visuals. Convenient and discreet, the Internet is also a great medium for purchasing literature and sex toys. ♥

5

Tickle Your Fancy

6 Lubrication

Women vary greatly in the amount of natural wetness their bodies produce. Whether your body produces abundant amounts of natural lubrication or you remain relatively dry when aroused, lubrication, or "lube," can greatly enhance a sexual self-pleasuring session. There's no need to rely solely on your own natural juices, as lubrication makes for safer and more comfortable stimulation. Basically, it allows for enhanced sensitivity when stroking or penetrating erogenous zones and provides a smooth and slippery surface. In addition, using lubrication helps women with vaginal dryness as sometimes caused by oral contraceptives, menopause, new motherhood, medication and more. If you're concerned about your lack of natural lubrication, contact your doctor.

Saliva

Your mouth provides its own form of lubrication: saliva! Use your finger to transfer saliva to your genitals and create a slippery surface. Saliva can also quickly reactivate previously applied lubrication. But remember that even saliva might not be enough lubrication, depending on your technique and choice of sex toys.

Water-Based Lubricants

Water-based lubricants are slick, non-irritating, non-staining, water-soluble, odorless and usually tasteless. These popular, thin and liquidy lubricants are great for vaginal play because they have a consistency similar to natural vaginal fluids and are easily washed off toys and the body.

Jelly Lubricants

Jelly lubricants have the same properties and advantages of water-based lubricants, but feel more like hair gel or jelly. These thicker lubricants are popular for anal play because they provide extensive lubrication and dry up less quickly than thinner lubricants.

Lubrication Tips ...

♥ Oil-based products such as cooking oils, petroleum jelly, hand lotions and creams weren't made for sexual purposes and shouldn't be used as lubrication. Oils aren't water-soluble and can provoke vaginal infections.

♥ Some lubes vary in consistency and texture from brand to brand. Luckily, sample sizes and small bottles make them easier to try. Explore different lubes to determine what works best for you.

♥ Lubrication can contain Nonoxynol-9 (N-9), an active ingredient in spermicide thought to prevent HIV transmission. However, recent studies by the Center for Disease Control prove that N-9 does not protect you against HIV. In fact, it can be highly irritating and create open pathways in a woman's body, actually facilitating the transfer of HIV.

♥ Lubricants also come in a variety of tasty and playful flavors. However, flavoring agents sometimes cause irritation. When playing solo, flavored lubes should be avoided.

Tickle Your Fancy

♥ Lubrication is absolutely necessary during anal play. Unlike the vagina, the anus doesn't produce natural lubrication.

♥ Lubrication should be used when inserting anything larger than a finger into the vagina.

♥ As a rule of thumb, you can never use too much lube. So get slippery!

7 Clitoral Stimulation

Using your fingers to stimulate the clitoris is a fundamental skill for masturbation. It's important to get familiar with your clitoris and learn the stroking styles that work best for you. As you develop this skill, concentrate on increasing your state of arousal and observe the sensations your clitoris produces. With proper stimulation, the clitoris' small head, underneath the clitoral hood, will swell with blood and begin to appear. The more aroused you get, the more erect and visible the head becomes. Once the clitoris is clearly erect and visible, you're on your way to orgasm.

Using your hands, you can stimulate your clitoris with combinations of various strokes. By using one or more fingers in pleasurable motions, delicately explore yourself and note the different levels of enjoyment that each technique produces. Experiment to determine your own specific taste.

Clitoral Stroking Styles ...

up and down, side to side. Begin your clitoral stimulation with basic movements: up and down, side to side. Place a finger or two softly on your clitoris and explore, using various amounts of pressure. Stroke up and down, side to side, becoming familiar with each of your inner vulva's unique crevices and soft skin folds. Discover your most sensitive spots.

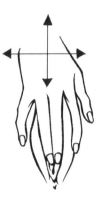

rolling between fingers. Place your thumb and index finger around the clitoris, then gently squeeze and lift it. Delicately roll it between your fingers. Start with a soft, slow roll, gradually picking up the pace and pressure. Explore light pinches and tugs to see how your clitoris reacts to each of these sexual sensations.

circular rub. Almost anyone can enjoy the circular technique. Place two fingers side by side over the top of your clitoris. Apply desired pressure and rub over your clitoris in circular motions. Experiment with varying the speed and pressure, using small to large circles. Once you perfect this technique, you may orgasm very quickly.

figure eights. The figure eight is a favorite of many women. Use one or more fingers to glide up, over and around your clitoral area in figure eights. Use small figures, focusing on the tip of your clitoris, or larger figures, stimulating the entire clitoris and inner labia. You can even get creative and rub your way through the alphabet!

three-fingers technique. This technique consists of rubbing your clitoris while using the same hand to hold the labia open. This method is great for freeing up a hand while you provide direct clitoral stimulation. Place your index finger and the finger next to your pinky on the top inside wall of the outer labia. Push and spread the labia against your body, holding the lips securely spread apart. Use your middle finger to stimulate your fully exposed clitoris, leaving your other hand free for sex toy play!

stroking the sides of the clitoris. Rub vertically along the sides of your clitoris for a delicately fine sensation. Place a fingertip on each side of your clitoris, sliding them up and down and back again. This will stimulate the clitoris as well as the sensitive inner labia.

massage. To fully cover the entire clitoris and inner labia, use the flat of your hand and fingers to massage. Take three or four fingers, side by side and flat, and snuggly position them between your outer labia. Apply pressure and stroke yourself using your favorite techniques.

tapping. Try tapping your clitoris to see if this technique is for you. Use one hand to gently separate your outer labia, fully exposing your clitoris. With your other hand, use your index finger to lightly tap on your clit. Increase the tapping speed and pressure to your delight.

light rub. Some women enjoy very light stimulation on only the tip of the clitoris. Enjoy this technique using any of the stroking styles while lightly rubbing the head of your clitoris for a more focused or "ticklish" feeling.

Clitoral Stimulation
playtime

*C*reate an environment to suit your mood and style. Lying on your back with your legs slightly spread apart, relax and let your mind go. Close your eyes and allow yourself to fantasize as you softly caress yourself. Generously apply lubrication to your entire vulva, including the clitoris, inner labia and outer labia. Or insert a finger into your vagina, transferring your natural lubrication to these areas.

Get familiar with your clitoris, exploring the unique sensations you create. Discover where you find the most pleasure. Use a fingertip to slowly rub the sides of your clit, getting familiar with its shape and sensitivity. Go from top to bottom and back again, stimulating the sensitive clitoral and inner labia nerve endings. Now slowly glide your fingertips side to side, back and forth over the tip of your clit. Do you feel a ticklish yet erotic, sexy feeling? Good. Now locate all the sensitive areas around the clitoris, including the commissure, clitoral hood and between the skin folds of your inner labia. Allow your pelvic muscles to tighten and release as your body reacts to the waves of pleasure you create. Continue to squeeze and release or "pump" your pelvic muscles as your sexual excitement builds. This can help your body produce natural lubrication, assist in building your orgasm and intensify your climax. Your journey to orgasm begins here.

Pick up the momentum as you rub your clit, experimenting with the manual clitoral stimulation techniques previously discussed in this chapter. Continue getting familiar with yourself. Try light rubbing on a particular spot, or a firm massage for a full area sensation. Stroking in circular motions can guarantee pleasure, but don't limit yourself—try them all! Alternate your stroking styles and vary the rhythm while applying different amounts of pressure and speed. Find where you are especially sensitive to touch and create your own masturbation style, incorporating your single, favorite technique or a combination.

Once you're familiar with your unique preferences of touch, speed and pressure, incorporate some playful variety. Try lightly

squeezing your clitoris from its base, rolling it between your finger-tips. Feel its unique shape and size while stroking the protruding tip with your other hand. Alternate between fast and slow, hard and soft combinations. Be creative and make it a personal, unique art. Try using one or more fingers and spelling the alphabet! Whatever your style, take time to linger over the sensations you are inducing. Remember, this is all about you.

Try to stimulate the clitoris to an erect state, where it "pops" out from under the hood and becomes clearly visible. Now, increase your speed while focusing on your clit and building toward orgasm.

Continue to directly stimulate the clitoris and surrounding area, but don't forget to breathe. You can breathe slowly, taking in deep breaths and exhaling fully, or hold your breath for a few moments and let it out with a big sigh. Alternatively, your style might favor short panting

Approximately 80% of women require direct clitoral stimulation to achieve orgasm.

breaths. Move your hips in slow, sensuous ways. Be aware of what your entire body is feeling. As you stroke your clitoris, consider using your other hand to play with your nipples. Gently squeeze and roll your nipples between your thumb and index fingers, or tug them lightly. If possible, lick or suck your own nipples!

Close your eyes and focus on building your orgasm, rubbing rapidly with consistent movements and firm pressure. Rhythmically pump your pelvic muscles, squeezing and releasing them with your hip movements. Continue stimulation with faster strokes and more pressure. Some signals that indicate an oncoming orgasm are strong tingling feelings in your clitoris, sporadic pelvic muscle contractions, increased wetness and heavier breathing.

Squeeze and hold the pelvic muscles as the orgasmic feelings approach. Concentrate on the build-up and bring it on. Continue until you have to let go! Keep pumping your pelvic muscles as you stroke yourself right into a breathtaking orgasm!

Don't slow the speed and pressure until after the first orgasmic contraction subsides, then ride out your orgasm as your pelvic muscles involuntarily contract. Switch your stroking styles to find one that brings you the most pleasurable feelings throughout your orgasmic contractions. If it feels good, you can continue stimulating your clitoris, but go slower and softer because your clit can get very sensitive during and after orgasm. Focus on your pelvic muscle and involuntary orgasmic contractions until every last one has been enjoyed! ♥

8 Dildos and Vaginal Penetration

Some women enjoy a perfectly satisfying sex life with little or no vaginal penetration. For others, the vagina is a great source of pleasure. Many women have vaginal orgasms, enjoying the pleasurable feelings of pressure, sexual fullness or stroking from penetration of a penis, finger or sex toy.

Dildos are non-vibrating toys, made in many different shapes and sizes, used for vaginal and anal penetration. A dildo exists for virtually every individual taste, need and desire. Some dildos realistically look like penises, others look like torpedoes and some non-realistic ones look like animals or vegetables. Dildos are generally made of silicone, latex, vinyl or rubber and vary in shape, color, texture and function. Silicon dildos are resilient, retain body heat and are easily cleaned, ranked among the highest quality dildos.

45

Tickle Your Fancy

Dildos come finger-sized or as large as an arm! Some are manufactured with a flared base or handles, allowing for an easy grip. Dildos are measured according to length and thickness. Length is measured from the

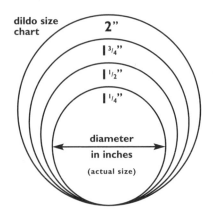

dildo size chart

2"

1³/₄"

1¹/₂"

1¹/₄"

diameter
in inches
(actual size)

base to the tip, but thickness is measured at the widest point. Exploring different dildos can introduce you to pleasurable feelings you may never have experienced. You never know what will turn you on until you try. After you've mastered masturbation with one dildo, try a slightly larger size and enjoy the newly enhanced feeling of fullness.

Dildos and Vaginal Penetration
play time

*G*et cozy and comfortable. Lay on your back, letting yourself get into a very relaxed state. Let your mind take its own direction, releasing all inhibitions or fears and mentally preparing yourself for sexual self-pleasure. Generously apply lubrication to your entire vulva, including the clitoris, inner and outer labia and vagina. Warm yourself up with your favorite manual clitoral stimulation technique and tease yourself. Build sexual excitement. Gently caress your clitoris, labia and vaginal entrance to make them warm, slightly swollen and erect. Awaken all your senses, softly stroking your breasts and playing with your nipples until they become hard. Notice as natural lubrication moistens your vagina and you become sexually aroused.

Begin penetration by applying lube to a finger and delicately inserting it into your vagina. Feel the tightness, softness and warmth of your vagina surrounding your finger. Continue to stroke and pleasure your clitoris with the other hand. Gently glide your finger in and out, getting familiar with the feelings of your insides. Stay with a slow and moderate pace. Insert your finger as far as you can reach, then back out. Close your eyes and enjoy the sensations of your fingertips gliding in and out of your vagina. Notice the erotic feelings you have created with your own touch and thrust. Squeeze and release your pelvic muscles, feeling their strength as they wrap around your finger.

After you get comfortable with one finger, try using two or more, varying your speed and style. Move straight in and out or softly press around inside and against the vaginal walls. Or, try twisting your fingers in a corkscrew motion. Throughout your session, remember to squeeze and pump your pelvic muscles, building toward orgasm.

Sex toys can be warmed between body parts such as your inner thighs and breasts, or by running the toys under hot water.

Dildos and Vaginal Penetration

After bringing yourself to a comfortable level of sexual arousal with clitoral stimulation and finger penetration, apply lube to your dildo. Tease the vaginal entrance with the tip of your dildo before carefully easing the dildo inside your vagina. Continue clitoral stimulation with your other hand while you enjoy dildo play. Massage the entire clitoral area, or use the "three-fingers technique" (see Chapter 7) to better focus on the clitoris.

Use the same penetration techniques with your dildo as you did with your finger. You are stimulating nerve endings as you stroke and penetrate your vaginal canal. Different depths generate different feelings, so feel free to experiment. You may prefer soft penetration, inserting only halfway and stroking slowly. Or you may like deep penetration, thrusting your toy in as far as it can go, creating feelings of pressure and being "filled up." Explore tipping your hips at different angles to create unique sensations in different parts of your vagina and vulva.

Another technique that stimulates the clitoris during vaginal penetration play is to tilt the dildo at a downward angle against your clitoris and vulva, gliding it in and out of your vagina. To do this, angle the dildo so that each back and forth stroke into the vagina slides between the labia and over the clitoris. This technique works best with a very flexible dildo and provides both clitoral and vaginal stimulation at the same time.

"Straddling" the dildo on top of a pillow pile is another great technique to explore. Stack several pillows into a mound big enough

Tickle Your Fancy

to snuggly straddle. Lay a towel over the pillows before straddling the mound. Place the dildo underneath yourself and let it glide up inside of you. As you then sit on and straddle the dildo, the pillows underneath will provide a base to push down against, as well as provide a cushion for you to wrap your legs around. This simulates the cowgirl position. Move and grind as if you're having sex on top. This technique takes some practice, so give yourself time to perfect your positioning, pillow stacking and so forth. Once you get your rhythm and balance down, add clitoral stimulation for an overall pleasurable experience.

Dildos and Vaginal Penetration

Remember that the clitoris contains most of your orgasmic nerve endings, so you'll usually need clitoral stimulation to orgasm during dildo play. Fine tune your clitoral stimulation, dildo stroking styles and positioning until you find your exact preference. Let your body move with its natural sexual rhythms. Circle your hips in small up and down motions, flexing and releasing your pelvic muscles with your rhythm and strokes. Let loose and vocalize what your body is feeling. Try moaning or talking out loud. Hearing yourself verbalize your enjoyment with phrases such as "Mmmmmmm" or "Oooh, that feels gooood!" can be a huge turn-on!

Since longer periods of sexual arousal often produce stronger, more invigorating orgasms, take your time while playing with yourself. There's no rush. Slowly build to your orgasm. Play fast, then slow. When you are ready for orgasm, speed up the clitoral stimulation. Concentrate on your masturbation techniques and physical state. Focus on the clitoral sensations of the approaching climax as you pump your pelvic muscles. Once orgasm begins, you can pump your dildo vigorously, thrusting it completely inside for a full feeling, or take it out and enjoy the orgasmic contractions of clitoral stimulation! ♥

Tickle Your Fancy

9 Vibrators

Vibrators can give intense pleasure to the clitoris and vulva and are among the strongest and most consistent forms of stimulation. Such electric and battery operated vibrators come in different shapes and sizes, often with multi-speeds and a variable control so you can change the intensity to suit your pleasure.

Vibrators can lightly massage muscles and body parts or directly stimulate your erogenous zones. Many women achieve intense orgasms much quicker with vibrators than by using manual methods. Vibrators also help create a powerful build-up to orgasm, letting you finish with another technique. You might be satisfied with another reliable method for achieving orgasm, but variety is the spice of life, so why not give it a try? When using vibrators, apply the same clitoral stroking techniques discussed in Chapter 7.

> Shannon, an 18-year-old college freshman, just recently decided to explore masturbation even though she started becoming aroused in her early teens. Books, magazine articles and underwear catalogues piqued her sexual interest. She often felt a growing warmth and tingling sensation in her vagina. Sometimes, she fell asleep with her hand drifting toward her panties. She heard about orgasms but wasn't sure if she had experienced one. This year, she earnestly sought information about "The Big O." Every women's magazine on the rack seemed to discuss the topic, but none offered any techniques. She swallowed her fear and visited a sex toy shop to look for toys. Disguised in a baseball cap and sunglasses, she pretended to be looking for a bachelorette gift for a "friend." To her surprise, the vibrator she purchased was a lot more rigid and intense than she expected, but with practice and patience, Shannon learned how to please herself sexually using her vibrator. She now experiences multiple orgasms with her new toy!

Shannon overcame her fears and used a vibrator to discover a whole new world of pleasure and multiple orgasms. A vibrator's looks and strength can be intimidating, but go on an adventure and explore your options to sexual pleasure!

Coil-Operated and Wand Vibrators

Coil-operated and wand electric vibrators provide extreme pleasure to the entire body, not just the clitoris. Coil-operated vibrators provide focused and steady vibrations and usually come packaged with four to six small attachments for playful variety. Wand vibrators are much larger and generate penetrating and diffuse vibrations. Wands also have soft, large vibrating heads that are the size of a tennis ball. Pre-orgasmic women often find wands more helpful than other vibrators because a wand's stimulation is much more intense. Commonly marketed as "personal muscle massagers," wands are widely available in sex toy shops, department stores and lingerie stores.

wand vibrator

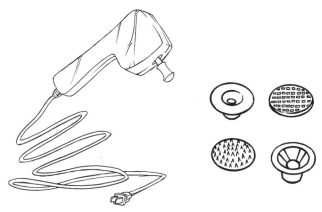

coil-operated vibrator and attachments

**One study found 26%
of women age 18 to 35 have
used a vibrator at least once.**

Battery-Operated Vibrators

Battery-operated vibrators are among the most popular sex toys available. Offered in many different shapes, sizes and colors, battery-operated vibrators are popular for being portable, versatile and cost effective. They're usually made of hard plastic, pliable vinyl or jelly rubber, designed to externally stimulate the clitoris or internally stimulate for vaginal and anal play. An assortment of attachments and jelly rubber sleeves allow you to change the shape and texture of your vibrator. Sleeves can make your vibrator vaginally or anally insertable, providing a new tingly sensation. Lightweight and easily portable vibrators are also ideal for carrying in your purse!

> ***mini-massagers.*** Battery-operated mini-massagers are a definite treat. Compact, easily portable, powerful and discreet, mini-massagers come with a selection of clitoral attachments. Fully waterproof mini-massagers are available and great for water play. A mini-massager can be your best travelling companion!

Vibrators

John Keough of Los Angeles applied for the first patent on an electrical vaginal vibrator in 1911. It was granted in 1912, patent No. 1,032,840.

egg-shaped. Vibrating egg-shaped stimulators or "bullets" are a little smaller than a real egg, attached by a thin cord to a battery pack. These vibrators are designed for vaginal insertion, but are commonly used topically for external clitoral stimulation. Such egg-shaped vibrators are aesthetically pleasing, small and available in attractive colors.

cylindrical. Cylindrical vibrators are one of the most commonly used types of vibrators. Some realistically resemble a penis while others have a smooth shape. Either way, cylindrical vibrators provide a steady stream of external and internal stimulation. They range in size from four to eight inches long and are usually about 1.25 inches in diameter. Many of these vibrators have a variable speed control at the base and sometimes come in kits.

Vibrators
play time

*G*ather your favorite lubrication and electric vibrator, then pick a location where you'd like to play. A love seat, chair or couch near an electrical outlet would be convenient. Get into the mood by massaging your inner thighs and vulva with your hands, caressing the areas you will glide the vibrator across. Become completely relaxed as you prepare your mind and body for sexual self-pleasure.

Turn on your electric vibrator and glide it over your inner thighs. Play around with different styles of movement and pressure. Explore your vibrator's different speeds and get familiar with its strength. After

you have a good feel for your vibrator, place its head against your vulva. Start stimulation on the outer labia and slowly glide the vibrator inward over the clitoris. Focus on clitoral stimulation, holding the vibrator with light, steady pressure and moving it in small, circular motions. To be neat and clean or to diffuse intense vibrations, wear panties or place a towel between your vulva and the vibrator. Squeeze and hold your pelvic muscles and focus on the enjoyable "tingly" sensations, fighting any ticklish feelings you may have. If this is your first time using a vibrator, be patient and give yourself time to practice and learn what feels good.

Move the vibrator over the surrounding areas such as your clitoral hood, vaginal and anal openings and labia. Stimulating these areas can be quite pleasurable and will often stimulate your clitoris indirectly.

Vibrators

Explore new sensations by varying the motion, alternating between hard and light pressure. Tease yourself by stopping, then starting again. You may want to stop and hold back if you feel an orgasm approaching. This can create different feelings, including a more intense orgasm later on. Enjoy the vibrations and energizing feelings the vibrator sends throughout your body. Incorporate vaginal finger stimulation, adding pleasure to the overall experience. Once comfortable, you can explore other positions. Try it standing or place your vibrator on top of a pillow to straddle and ride as if you're having sex on top. Control your experience and build up high levels of sexual tension before letting yourself go.

When you've had enough play and you're ready for orgasm, allow yourself to climax in one of many fun ways. Maintain direct clitoral stimulation with your vibrator up to and through orgasm. Go full force with clitoral stimulation, feeling your toes curl with each powerful contraction! If the vibration is too intense during orgasm, you can apply the "diffusion technique," placing three side-by-side fingers between the vibrator and your clitoris as you start to climax. This allows for continued stimulation of the clitoris, but with an overall softer vibration. You can then ride out your orgasmic contractions while maintaining direct clitoral stimulation.

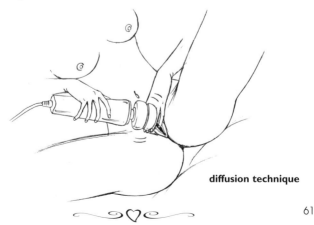

diffusion technique

Tickle Your Fancy

Another popular technique is bringing yourself to the point of orgasm with the vibrator, then quickly switching to manual clitoral stimulation as you begin to climax. Then let your orgasm go, riding it out with swift manual clitoral stimulation. Do you feel the unique euphoric rush created by interchanging the stimulation right before orgasm? After this orgasm, give yourself a short break, then keep going! Place the vibrator back onto your clitoral area and go for a second orgasm. Squeeze and hold your pelvic muscle to fight any ticklish feelings from your previous orgasm and concentrate—you'll probably find your next orgasm much easier to reach.

An altogether different orgasm can be reached by fully relaxing as you masturbate. Instead of flexing your pelvic muscles and concentrating on technique and orgasm, just relax. Don't focus on the orgasmic feelings you may be inducing as you play, just keep the vibrator on your clitoris. There will come a point when you feel your orgasm approaching. Don't stop the stimulation. When there's no holding back, let your body burst into an invigorating orgasm, enjoying each powerful contraction! ❤

10

G-spot
Play

G-spot stimulation is a great pleasure for some women; for others, it's a new, unexplored pleasure spot. If you're a newcomer to G-spot stimulation, don't be intimidated. This erogenous zone often needs lots of practice to successfully stimulate it, but the extra effort can be well worth your time. In addition to the G-spot, there's a range of possible pleasure spots that can be vaginally sensitive. Each woman's G-spot and pleasure areas will be uniquely situated. Some women even find the back of the vagina wall sensitive. Don't limit yourself to just one spot!

Tickle Your Fancy

g-spot vibrator   g-spot dildo with handle

Some sex toys, such as dildos and vibrators, are designed specifically for G-spot stimulation. The most common G-spot stimulator resembles a cylindrical vibrator but is slightly curved at the end of the shaft. This curved tip is angled to press up against a woman's G-spot when inserted vaginally. Some G-spot dildos have handles to help you apply firm, steady pressure against the G-spot. You may also enjoy flexible G-spot dildos that bend and shape to your body.

Some G-spot attachments fit over the head of wand electric vibrators, allowing for the insertable portion of the attachment to stimulate the vagina and G-spot. Meanwhile, the wand's vibrating head can be pressed against the clitoris.

G-spot Play

It can be difficult to achieve orgasm from G-spot stimulation alone, especially if you're newly exploring this area. Don't get discouraged. It could take weeks or months to become familiar with this erogenous zone and the unique pleasure it creates. As with the clitoris, you have to condition your G-spot to climax. While teaching your body to have G-spot orgasms, use other stimulation to provide additional pleasure. It's also important to use firm pressure, not a light touch, because the G-spot isn't in the vagina and instead gets stimulated through the vaginal wall.

Remember that the G-spot is located near the urethra, so stimulating the G-spot often produces the urge to urinate. Don't worry—it's a perfectly normal feeling.

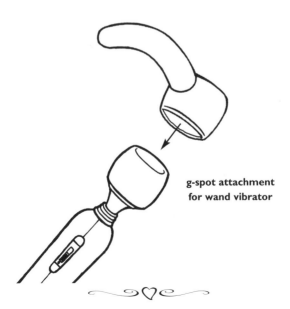

**g-spot attachment
for wand vibrator**

G-spot
play time

*S*tart by locating your G-spot to familiarize yourself with this erogenous zone. Generously apply lubrication to your vulva and middle fingers. In whatever position you are most comfortable, gently insert your fingers into your vagina a couple inches in from the vaginal entrance, and bend them toward the front wall in a "come here" finger position, applying pressure toward the pubic bone.

Tickle Your Fancy

Initially, the G-spot will feel like a small mass of rigid, firm tissue about the size of a dime. Stroke the upper vaginal wall with your finger, pressing around and feeling for this small mass of tissue. Remember: The vaginal canal doesn't have many nerve endings. When you experience new, unique feelings, you've likely found the G-spot.

The G-spot's location differs from woman to woman, so take your time and discover the location of your personal pleasure spot. Pay attention to the feelings you induce as you touch and explore. Be open to these feelings and learn to enjoy them. It could take many sessions of playing and experimenting with your G-spot to really feel these sensations from stimulation, so be patient. One or two fingers may not sufficiently stimulate the G-spot to become fully aroused. Some women need to be "filled up" with a G-spot dildo to enjoy it.

Take your G-spot dildo and apply lube to it. Let your mind travel to a comfortable and uninhibited state. Take a moment to play with yourself by engaging in manual clitoral stimulation or finger penetration. After you reach a heightened state of sexual arousal, slowly insert the G-spot dildo into your vagina with the curved tip pointing upward. Experiment with different strokes and pressure against the vaginal wall as you would with any type of penetration, getting familiar with this erogenous zone. Now apply extra pressure on the G-spot with the tip of the dildo fully inside, at the top and toward the belly. Remember, this unique pleasure spot requires firmer pressure and quick rubbing strokes, not in-and-out thrusting. Don't be alarmed if you feel the urge to urinate. As you feel your way through the different sensations while

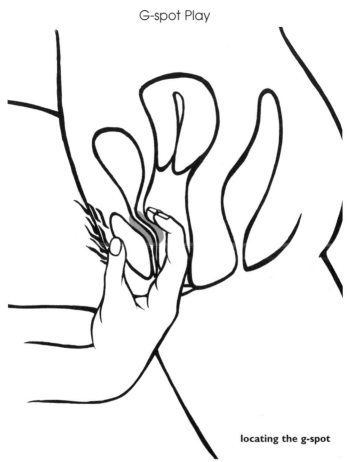

locating the g-spot

exploring your G-spot, use your other hand or a vibrator to incorporate clitoral stimulation. This combination of G-spot and clitoral stimulation creates pure delight for many women.

You can also enhance G-spot stimulation with pressure from the outside. While your G-spot dildo is snug inside and firmly rubbing against your G-spot, use the flat of your free hand to push down firmly on your abdomen (the lower stomach just above your pubic hair line). This is known as "external G-spot stimulation." The combination of internal and external pressure may be quite pleasurable.

Now pump away with your pelvic muscles, building toward orgasm. Close your eyes to fully feel and enjoy all the stimulation you're providing. Focus on the clitoris and the orgasmic feelings you're inducing. Again, since the clitoris is the main source of orgasm, adding this to G-spot play can help you achieve orgasm and intensify the overall experience.

As with all techniques, breathe in and exhale deeply while you build your orgasm. When you achieve orgasm, the added pleasure of G-spot stimulation may take your breath away. Some women feel as if they're having two types of orgasm at the same time. It's perfectly natural for some women to ejaculate when they climax from G-spot orgasms, so don't mistake this for urine. ♥

11
Anal
Play

Many women use anal stimulation during masturbation to enhance the overall experience. Some enjoy the simple pressure of a finger or thumb stroking the anal opening, while others prefer some form of penetration with fingers, dildos or a plug. Don't be intimidated by this region of your body. Contrary to myth, anal play isn't harmful. In fact, many women find anal play extremely pleasurable.

Tickle Your Fancy

Allow yourself to soak in the unique feelings anal play can induce. As with G-spot stimulation, keep in mind that you may not orgasm from this type of stimulation alone. But you can certainly enjoy the sensations that this activity elicits, contributing to a stronger, more exhilarating clitoral or vaginal orgasm.

Good etiquette, technique and style of play are crucial when stimulating this erotic zone. When using a finger or sex toy for anal play, don't insert it in your vagina until you've washed the item with anti-bacterial soap. Transferring bacteria from one area to another could cause infection. And remember, lubrication is absolutely necessary during anal play, because the anus, unlike the vagina, does not produce natural lubrication.

> *plugs.* Plugs are toys made for anal play, generally made of silicone, latex or vinyl. Plugs come in a variety of different sizes, but all have a similar shape—narrow at the base, thickest in the middle and narrowest on top. The flared base prevents the plug from getting lost or going too far inside the rectum. Plugs are made to rest still while inside rather than be pushed in and out. Wearing a plug helps train and relax the anal muscles, plus it provides a pleasurable feeling of fullness as you stimulate other erogenous zones.

Anal
play time

*B*egin your anal explorations by getting into a sensual mood. Try taking a warm bath to relax, get clean and prepare for fun. While in the tub, caress yourself and begin to arouse your entire body. After your bath, position yourself on a bed or couch and lie on your back with your knees bent, heels pulled up and feet flat. Or, you can stand with one foot propped on a chair. Basically, find a position that allows you to stimulate your clitoris while reaching your anus at the same time. Once you're comfortably positioned, relax all your muscles and concentrate on letting yourself go. Relax, relax, relax. Take several deep breaths while flexing and releasing your pelvic muscles, getting your body warmed up and your blood flowing. Gently massage your buttocks, inner thighs and the area around your anus. Continue to relax. Then, take your time and slowly rub lots of lubrication over your anal entrance.

Circle a lubricated fingertip around the soft folds of the anal entrance with a gentle touch. Rub, stroke, tease and play with it. Explore its softness and warmth. Notice how this part of your body contracts to the slightest touch as you glide your slippery finger over your skin. Stimulating the anal opening, which is full of nerve endings, can be extremely pleasurable. Completely relax all your anal muscles. This is very important during anal play, especially during penetration. Now use your finger to press gently at the opening. Continue touching and pressing until you feel ready for more. You can also use a vibrator to loosen up this area—the vibrations relax the area and get your blood pumping.

Stimulate your clitoris to build more sexual excitement and arousal. Use your fingers or a vibrator. If you like, switch to or add some vaginal penetration. You should feel yourself becoming more aroused—just play and enjoy yourself for a while. Now that you've gotten your clitoris and vagina worked up, tease this special erogenous zone again. Apply more lubrication to your finger. Explore penetration this time, probing gently with one fingertip. As you do this, completely relax and use your anal muscles to slightly "push out," just as when you have a bowel movement.

The anal muscles work in an opposite fashion as the vaginal muscles. While you "squeeze" the vaginal muscles with penetration, you "push out" with anal penetration, enabling the sphincter muscles to relax and contract to easily accept fingers or other objects. Slowly insert the tip of your finger into your anus and hold it there. Then go in up to mid-finger and hold it there. Let your anus get used to the feeling of having something inside it and allow the sphincter muscles to relax. Then slide your finger in a little further. Keep in mind that with

Anal Play

anal play, you don't need to insert the entire length of your finger or dildo, nor thrust as vigorously as you would vaginally. Feel the unique tightness of your sphincter muscles around your finger. Gently probe by working it in and out, starting at a slow pace. Work your way up to a nice, steady rhythm, thrusting your finger in and out at your own comfortable pace and depth. You can also play by circling your finger just inside the anal opening.

At this point, you may want to enhance play with a dildo or anal vibrator. Or, you could also use the "bowling ball" technique. This entails having an entire thumb inside your vagina, with a remaining finger inside your anus, much as you would hold a bowling ball. This technique provides a great feeling of sexual fullness and is wonderful to apply while stroking your clitoris. Whatever your preference, stick with a pleasurable technique and continue stroking your clitoris at the same time.

In most cases, as with G-spot stimulation, anal play is an "added pleasure" technique. Usually, it's a challenge to orgasm from anal stimulation alone, but it can greatly enhance your sexual experiences. Focus on enjoying the sexual feelings anal play can create and let the stimulation overwhelm you. When bringing yourself to climax, use your preferred clitoral stimulation technique. Speed up your strokes and concentrate on climaxing. At the same time, continue your anal play for an enhanced sexual sensation. Experience anal stimulation and enjoy the wild and erotic sensations it adds to your already powerful orgasms! ♥

12 Water Fun and Creative Objects

The bathroom is a great place to play and offers privacy from family and roommates. Water flow, especially when directed onto the clitoral area, can be extremely sensual and offers a variety of sexual self-pleasuring techniques. Also, water-resistant sex toys are made specifically for water play. Experience a special kind of eroticism by playing with water-resistant vibrators in the shower or bathtub!

bathtub faucet. Erotic play in the bathtub is one of the easiest ways for women to play at home. Most people have a water faucet and it's a simple technique to engage in.

Adjust the water to a comfortable temperature and fill the tub halfway. Lying on your back, bring your buttocks near the end of the tub with the faucet and bring your knees toward your chest. Position your vulva directly below the faucet and tilt your pelvis upward toward the water flow. Once comfortably positioned, use your hands to gently separate your labia so the water can flow directly onto your clitoris. Lie back, relax, fantasize and enjoy!

shower massagers. Adjust the temperature and pressure of the water to your liking and take the shower massager in your hand. If possible, place one foot up on the side of the tub or shower seat,

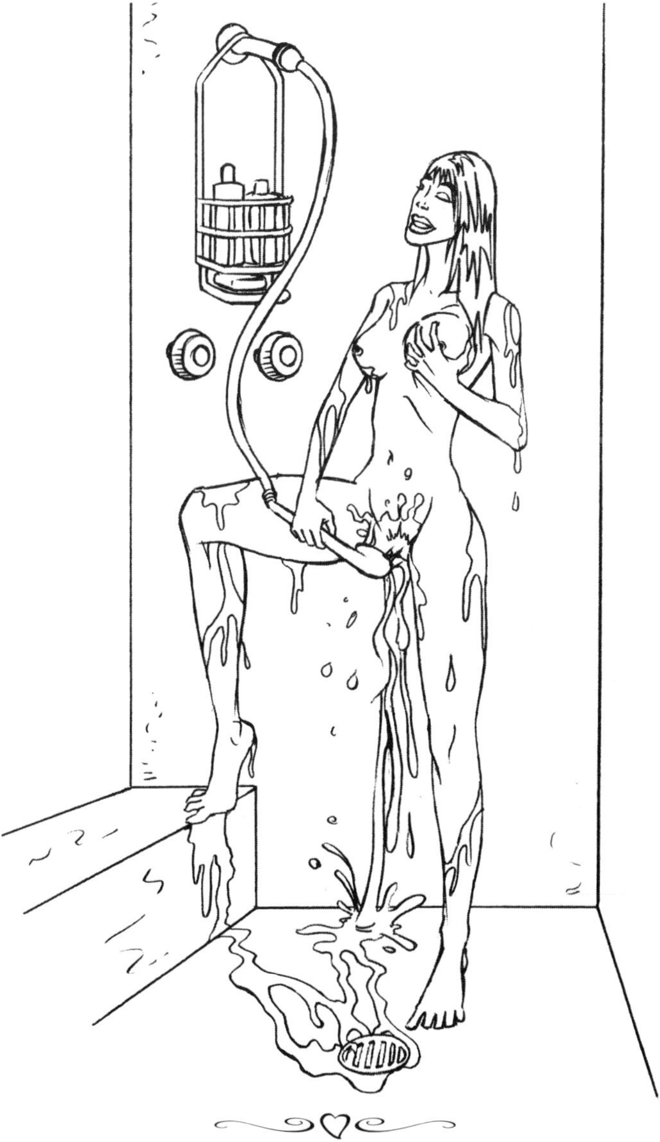

Using a shower massager is the third most common method in which women have discovered orgasm, right after manual stimulation and rubbing against an object. directing the water flow onto your clitoral area. The faster the water flow, the more stimulating the effect. Try starting with a low pressure, increasing it as you become more aroused. Be cautious with high levels of pressure or sending strong streams of water into the vagina, as either can cause irritation. For even more fun, use shower massagers with versatile control switches to alter the jet spray to your liking. Many women can achieve orgasm in a few minutes or less with this kind of direct clitoral stimulation.

jacuzzi jets. Take advantage of the strong water flow coming from jacuzzi jets! Hold onto the edge of the jacuzzi, placing both feet up on the wall. Put one foot on each side of the jet and straddle it. Or, turn around and back into it, letting the water flow from behind. Position your clitoral area directly in the path of the stream. Because a jacuzzi's water flow is much stronger than that of a shower or bathtub, start off a good distance from the jet and move closer until you find the most desirable pressure. Once you're the right distance from the jet, enjoy the soothing, warm water all over your body as the clitoris gets delightfully stimulated!

le bidet. Designed by the French for washing the more intimate body parts, the bidet makes for a convenient masturbation toy. If you're lucky enough to have access to a bidet, straddle the seat and position yourself above  the water faucet. Adjust the pressure of the water and enjoy the arousing feelings as it flows upward onto your clitoris. Now you're in a perfect position to incorporate manual clitoral stimulation with fingers or a water-resistant vibrator.

Creative Objects

When it comes to masturbation, there are no rules! In addition to traditional techniques and sex toys, other creative techniques exist. Open your playful imagination and adapt to some new ways to explore. Get creative using pillows, furniture and more.

However, always use caution and examine your play toys carefully for sharp edges or harmful surfaces. With the following techniques, consider keeping your underwear on as you play in case things get a little damp.

Tickle Your Fancy

pillow play. Pillows are convenient sex toys. Twist one corner into a knot and comfortably position yourself and vulva over the knot. Now roll your hips in small circular motions while adjusting your speed and pressure to your liking. Enjoy the overall stimulation this little knot has to offer and ride away until you bring yourself to orgasm!

sock play. Rolled socks are excellent toys, big enough to stimulate your clitoris, labia and vaginal opening at the same time. Roll a pair of tube socks into a larger sock. Place the sock on the bed beneath you and straddle it. Now roll your hips in small circles against its firmness. Try grasping it between your legs and feel the pressure against your inner thighs and anus as you roll around.

furniture. Rubbing against the corner of a piece of furniture can be a tactile delight. Couch arms and soft chair corners are popular. Even a bedpost can provide just the right size and feel. While your clitoris can likely withstand the pressure, your pelvic bone could become very sore. To avoid that discomfort, thrust your hips forward and tuck your pelvis under as you rub against hard surfaces. Also, consider placing a towel or small blanket between yourself and the surface to avoid dampness and harmful friction.

washing machine. Are you feeling adventurous? Try sitting on top of your washing machine during the spin cycle. You'll be surprised at how much pleasure its tremors produce! ♥

13

Cleanliness
and
Safety Tips

Be responsible with your body and keep your self-loving experiences safe. Remember: The vagina is a moist open area and susceptible to infection. Use proper hygiene and be careful with objects not designed for sexual stimulation.

~~∽♡∼~~   83

Tickle Your Fancy

💜 Your hands collect more bacteria than most parts of your body. Unwashed hands and toys can result in yeast and vaginal infections. Always wash your hands and sex toys thoroughly with anti-bacterial soap before and after each use.

💜 Vaginal and anal tissues are very delicate. When using your fingers, make sure your nails are short and filed smooth, with no jagged or sharp edges that could tear the tissue. If you have long nails, make them safe and soft by wrapping cotton around the tips, then put on latex gloves or "finger-cots" made for sexual play and protection.

💜 To reduce the risk of infection, use condoms on your sex toys and don't share them.

💜 Examine your toys carefully and thoroughly. If using creative objects not intended for masturbation, make sure there are no sharp, rough or jagged edges that could cut or break inside you.

💜 Clean dildos before and after each use with anti-bacterial soap. Sterilize your silicone dildos in boiling water. Dry washed toys completely before storing them.

💜 Wipe vibrators clean with a cloth moistened with warm water and anti-bacterial soap or an adult sex toy cleanser.

💜 Using a lubricated condom on penetrating objects reduces the risk of infection, plus helps protect your vaginal and anal lining from abrasion.

💜 Always urinate after sexual play to flush the urethral opening of any lubrication, fluids or bacteria that could cause infections. You may have difficulty urinating after orgasm because your body sometimes needs a moment to normalize after sexual arousal.

💜 When engaging in anal play, ALWAYS use lubrication and remember that the anal sphincter muscles contract and can suck objects inside. It is critical that anything you put in your anus (aside from a finger) has a flared base.

Conclusion

Masturbation is about loving and caring for yourself. It is a natural way of relating to your body and can be a romantic part of every woman's life.

Don't be afraid to try masturbation for the first time, perfect your techniques or explore new erogenous zones. Every individual has different sexual tastes, just as they have different tastes in music, clothes and perfume. There is no "right" way to enjoy sexual pleasure and orgasm, so you can always build your sexual self-pleasuring skills and explore new horizons.

Even after you find a favorite method, continue to experiment. Learn as much as you can about your body. You can discover unexpected ways to turn yourself on, finding different techniques to produce different reactions. Never stop striving to explore and enjoy your body. Once you get started, practice, practice, practice! Masturbate often. And remember—there's no need to worry about what others think. Masturbation is a private experience for you and you alone.

Single or married, young or old, masturbation might be the key to a consistently fulfilling sex life. You have nothing to lose by experimenting with masturbation and sex toys. In fact, it's likely you'll enter a new realm of pleasure. Explore your sexuality, release your inhibitions and enjoy your self-loving! ❤

About
the
Author

Sadie Allison graduated from San Diego State University with a bachelor's degree in French and Marketing. While working in the high-pace, high-tech sales industry in Silicon Valley, Sadie constantly advised her friends on their sex lives and realized the constant need for education on women's sexuality issues. *Tickle Your Fancy* reflects three years of sexuality research on Sadie's part, and is the first in a series of sexual "how-to" books from Tickle Kitty Press, her publishing company.

Special
Thanks

I'd like to thank my family and friends for fueling me with the endless encouragement, faith, love and support that helped me bring *Tickle Your Fancy* to life - especially Mom, Jason J., Justin J., Joshua J., Jazmin J., Kristin L., Jason K. and Luciano G.

And a very special thanks to Richard M., David A., and Steve L. for their hours of dedicated, hard work on the book's creative development.

Finally, I'd like to thank the pioneers in the field of female masturbation and sexuality who remain an inspiration, including: Joani Blank, Betty Dodson and Eve Ensler. This list is by no means complete, but credit should also be given to authors, sex-positive organizations and publishers, including: Laura Corn, Lonnie Barbach, Susie Bright, Barbara Keesling, Anne Semans, Tristan Taormino, Carol Queen, Cathy Winks, San Francisco Sex Information, Society for Human Sexuality, the team at Good Vibrations, Greenery Press, Down There Press, Cleis Press and Feminist Health Press.

Bibliography

Barbach, Lonnie G. For Yourself: The Fulfillment of Female Sexuality, New American Library, 1991.

Chichester, Brian and Robinson, Kenton. Sex Secrets: Ways to Satisfy Your Partner Every Time, Rodale Press, 1996.

Davidowitz, Esther. "Private Pleasures," Redbook, Vol. 18, Issue 1, Nov. 1992.

Dodson, Betty. Sex for One: The Joy of Selfloving, Three Rivers Press, 1996.

Federation of Feminist Women's Health Centers, A New View of a Woman's Body, Feminist Health Press, 1991.

Heiman, Julia R. Becoming Orgasmic—A Sexual and Personal Growth Program for Women, Simon & Schuster Inc., 1988.

Hite, Shere. The Hite Report: A Nation Wide Study of Female Sexuality, Macmillan Publishing, 1976.

Joannides, Paul. The Guide to Getting it On, Second Edition, Goofy Foot Press, 1999.

Keesling, Barbara. Sexual Pleasure, Reaching New Heights of Sexual Arousal and Intimacy, Hunter House Publications, 1993.

Kinsey, Alfred C.; Pomeroy, Wardell B.; Martin, Clyde E.; and Gebhard, Paul H. Sexual Behavior in the Human Female, W.B. Saunders Company, 1953.

Levins, Hoag. American Sex Machines—The Hidden History of Sex at the U.S. Patent Office, Adams Media Corporation, 1996.

Masters, William H. and Johnson, Virginia E. Human Sexual Response, Lippincott Williams & Wilkins Publishers, 1966.

McCoy Ph.D., Kathy. and Wibbelsman M.D., Charles. The Teenage Body Book, Perigee, 1999.

Moglia Ed.D, Ronald. All About Sex & Sexuality, Planned Parenthood Books, Three Rivers Press, 1997.

Paget, Lou. How to Give Her Absolute Pleasure—Totally Explicit Techniques Every Woman Wants Her Man to Know, Broadway Books, 2000.

Quilliam, Susan. Women on Sex, Barricade Books, 1995.

Reuben, David R. Everything You Always Wanted to Know About Sex But Were Afraid to Ask, Harper Collins, 1999.

Taormino, Tristan. The Ultimate Guide to Anal Sex for Women, Cleis Press, 1998.

Winks, Cathy. The Good Vibrations Guide: The G-Spot, Down There Press, 1998.

Winks, Cathy and Semans, Anne. The New Good Vibrations Guide to Sex, Second Edition, Down There Press, 1997.

Tickle Your Fancy

www.ticklekitty.com

Order more copies of *Tickle Your Fancy: A Woman's Guide to Sexual Self-Pleasure!*

There's three easy ways to order!

Order online at ticklekitty.com

or

Photocopy form, mail with check or money order

or

Fax credit card info to (415) 876-1900

PLEASE PRINT CLEARLY:

Name _____ Date ___/___/___

Mailing Address _____

City _____ State/Province _____

Zip/Postal Code _____ Country _____

Phone (___) _____ Email _____

Credit Card # _____ Exp Date ___/___/___

Signature _____

Payment in US $ only. ❑ Visa ❑ MasterCard ❑ Check/Money Order

Make check or money order payable to "Tickle Kitty Press" and mail to:

Tickle Kitty Press
3701 Sacramento Street
PMB #107
San Francisco, CA 94118
United States

Are you:
❑ FEMALE
❑ MALE
BIRTHDATE ___/___/___

Prices include shipping and handling.		
United States residents: Quantity____ × $15.95	=	$.
International residents: Quantity____ × $17.95	=	$.
8.5% sales tax for CA state residents	=	$.
Total	=	$.

How did you hear about *Tickle Your Fancy?* _____